I0143361

FURRY FRIENDS AND SIKH WISDOM

Psalm Carnoustie

To all the curious little explorers,

May your hearts always be brave like lions,
Your words kind like the gentle breeze,
And your spirits bright like the Golden Temple at sunrise.

This book is for you—the adventurers, the dreamers, and the little heroes who will carry kindness, courage, and love wherever you go.

Let these stories be your guide, your joy, and your reminder that every small act of goodness makes the

world a little brighter.

With love and a sprinkle of magic,
Psalm Carnoustie

Copyright 2025 by Psalm Carnoustie

All rights reserved.

No portion of this book may be reproduced in any form without written permission from the publisher or author, except as permitted by U.S. copyright law.

This publication is designed to provide accurate and authoritative information in regard to the subject matter covered. It is sold with the understanding that neither the author nor the publisher is engaged in rendering legal, investment, accounting or other professional services. While the publisher and author have used their best efforts in preparing this book, they make no representations or warranties with respect to the accuracy or completeness of the contents of this book and specifically disclaim any implied warranties of merchantability or fitness for a particular purpose. No warranty may be created or extended by sales representatives or written sales materials. The advice and strategies contained herein may not be suitable for your situation. You should consult with a professional when appropriate. Neither the publisher nor the author shall be liable for any loss of profit or any other commercial damages, including but not limited to special, incidental, consequential, personal, or other damages.

Book Cover by Tukotuku Publishing

Illustrations by Tukotuku Publishing

First edition 2025

Print ISBN: 978-1-991339-37-9

Ebook ISBN: 978-1-991339-38-6

TU
KO
TU
KU PUBLISHING

Contents

Welcome to Furry Friends & Sikh Wisdom

Animal Tales with Timeless Lessons!

Welcome, Little Explorer!

Hi there, bright-eyed adventurer! Are you ready to jump into a world where animals chatter, courage shines, and kindness is the biggest superpower of all? Then grab your favorite cozy blanket or your wiggliest stuffed bunny—because it's time to leap into Furry Friends & Sikh Wisdom!

This isn't just any storybook. Nope! It's like a magical treasure box filled with talking animals, exciting adventures, and big-hearted lessons inspired by Sikh teachings. Sikhism is all about being kind, brave, helpful, and sharing your last cookie (even if it's chocolate chip). Whether you've got feathers, fur, or funny dance moves—everyone's invited.

You'll meet some amazing new friends:

A wise old owl who gives the best advice (and hoots at the right moment!)

A silly monkey who finds out sharing isn't so bad after all (especially when bananas are involved)

A lion who teaches us that real bravery isn't loud—it's full of love! And a teeny squirrel who proves that even the smallest paws can do BIG things.

But these aren't just stories to make you giggle (though there will be plenty of giggles). Each one is packed with timeless lessons about helping others, standing up for what's right, and being your awesome, kind self—just like Sikh heroes have done for centuries.

You'll also get to celebrate Sikh festivals, learn about amazing traditions, and meet real-life heroes who made the world better with their courage, faith, and friendly hearts. Think of this book as your magical map—leading you through tales where furry friends and Sikh wisdom join paws to light the way.

So whether you're snuggled up in bed, reading on a sunny picnic blanket, or sharing the stories with your favorite grown-up or teddybear—get ready for a journey full of laughter, love, and a few happy surprises.

Alright, brave explorer—turn the page and let's dive into a world where kindness is powerful, friendship is forever, and every tail comes with a tale.

Let the adventures begin!

The World of Sikhs

What is Sikhism?

A Hug of Kindness, Courage, and Community!

Sikhism is like a big rainbow-colored umbrella that brings everyone together underneath—kids, grown-ups, and even the giggliest squirrels! It all began a long time ago in India with a cheerful explorer named Guru Nanak, who asked big questions and gave even bigger hugs (the cozy kind that make you feel all warm inside). He believed everyone—whether tall like a giraffe or tiny like a mouse—deserves kindness, friendship, and a whole lot of sharing. Even snacks! Because let's be real—what's better than sharing a cookie with your best friend? (Or your dog, if you're feeling extra generous!)

Now let's meet some Sikh superheroes! They might not wear capes, but they definitely wear courage in their hearts. Take Bhagat Singh, for example—a brave heart with the roar of a lion and the smarts of a curious cat. Sikh heroes are like the wise owl who protects the forest or the brave little bunny who stands up to the grumpy badger. They teach us that standing up for what's right doesn't need superpowers—just a super heart.

And oh, the celebrations! Sikh festivals like Vaisakhi and Gurpurab are one big, beautiful parade of colors, music, and... yummy food! Picture the whole forest coming together for a party: deer dancing, birds singing, and bears serving sweets with their big paws. There's enough halwa and kheer for everyone—even that sneaky raccoon who always shows up late! These festivals remind us that when we celebrate together, our joy grows like sunflowers in the spring.

In the Sikh world, community means everything. Think of bees buzzing together to make golden honey or penguins huddling up to stay warm—that's the Sikh spirit! Whether it's serving meals at Langar (the community kitchen), planting trees, or helping someone carry their backpack, every good deed adds a little sparkle to the world. Like a helpful elephant guiding a lost chick home, Sikh stories show that big hearts come in all shapes, sizes, and stripes!

And guess what? Sikh teachings love animals and nature just as much as kids love story time. There are tales of chatty parrots, helpful foxes, and thoughtful turtles who teach lessons about sharing, listening, and being brave. Whether it's a monkey learning patience or a kind squirrel building homes for birds, every story leaves behind a twinkle of wisdom. In Sikhism, even the tiniest pawprint can leave the biggest impact.

So as you explore the wonderful world of Sikh stories, get ready to giggle, learn, and maybe hug a few imaginary animals along the way. Because Sikhism is all about living with love, helping with heart, and dancing through life with friends by your side—even the furry, feathered kind!

Meet Guru Nanak

The First Guru

Little Nanak and the Giggle That Changed the World

Once upon a giggle—yes, a giggle—in a cozy little village called Talwandi, a baby named Nanak was born. But Nanak wasn't your usual peekaboo-loving baby. Oh no! Instead of crying, he smiled at the sun, waved at the birds, and let out the happiest laugh that tickled everyone's hearts. Even the cows gathered around like curious fans, mooing as if to say, "Who's this tiny human with the magical giggle?"

As Nanak grew, he didn't play with toy trains or shiny marbles. Nope—he made friends with butterflies, goats, and even chatty squirrels! He'd sit under a big shady tree, nibbling his snacks and handing crumbs to his fluttery, furry buddies. One day, he spotted a flock of geese flying perfectly in a V-shape across the sky. "Hey!" Nanak shouted, "Why do you all fly like that?" A wise goose honked back, "We fly together so we don't get lost. We help each other along the way." Nanak beamed. "Helping each other? That's genius!" And from then on, helping became one of his favorite things to do.

One sunny morning, Nanak saw a farmer struggling to plow his field. "Looks like you need a team," Nanak said, scratching his head thoughtfully. So what did he do? He gathered all his animal pals—cows to pull the plow, chickens to cheer them on, and rabbits to bounce around with snacks! In no time, the field was ready. The farmer clapped with joy. "That's the power of team-work!" Nanak grinned, and the animals high-fived... or rather, high-hooved and high-pawed!

Pretty soon, everyone in the village began stopping by to hear Nanak's stories. He didn't just talk—he told tales with laughter, adventure, and a sprinkle of silliness. "If a lion can share his den with a mouse," he'd say, "surely we can share our hearts with others." The crowd would roar with giggles (yes, even the goats!)

while learning big lessons in small words—be kind, be fair, and always care.

And guess what? That cheerful little boy grew up to become Guru Nanak, the very first Sikh Guru! But he didn't stop there. He traveled to faraway lands with nothing but love in his pocket and kindness in his heart, meeting people from all walks of life. He sang songs under the stars, hugged trees, and celebrated with friends new and old—reminding everyone that the world is better when we dance, laugh, and help one another.

So the next time you hear a giggle that makes you smile, it might just be the spirit of Nanak reminding you that a kind heart and a brave smile can change the world—one furry friend, one shared snack, and one silly story at a time.

The Lesson?
Even the tiniest giggle can spark something big! Guru Nanak showed us that kindness, team-work, and joy aren't just for grown-ups—they start with lit-tle acts of love, just like shar-ing snacks or helping a friend. So be like Nanak: laugh loud, help often, and spread kindness like

sunshine. You never know—your happy heart might just change the world too!

The Importance of the Sikh Community

The Sikh Spirit

One Big Patchwork of Love

In a cozy corner of the world, there's a community that shines as brightly as a basket of glittery marbles. It's called the Sikh community, and it's like a giant quilt—stitched together with patches of kindness, bravery, and giggles galore! Each piece tells a story, and when you snuggle into it, you feel warm, safe, and ready for adventure.

Now, imagine a squirrel scampering around, gathering nuts to share with its friends. That's how Sikhs work too—always collecting good deeds and passing them around like candy on Diwali! Whether they're cooking a giant pot of lentils to feed others or planting trees so birds can sing in the shade, Sikhs know that when everyone helps out, magic happens.

And oh, how they celebrate! Picture this: a big street parade with people dancing the bhangra, kids twirling ribbons, and music so joyful that even the pigeons bop along! During special days like Vaisakhi, the Sikh community throws the kind of party that even the moon peeks out early to watch. Everyone laughs, eats sweet treats, and shares stories like one big, happy family.

But wait—every party has its superheroes, right? In the

Sikh world, heroes don't wear capes—they wear courage and kindness! They might not fly, but they sure can stand tall for what's right. If someone's being left out or needs a hand, Sikh heroes step in faster than a monkey spotting a banana! Just like a little ant carrying a crumb three times its size, Sikh values show us that small actions can lead to BIG change.

And let's not forget nature—because in Sikh stories, the animals talk, the rivers sing, and the trees whisper secrets if you listen close. A clever rabbit might team up with a wise old turtle to clean up the forest, or a lion might roar, not to scare, but to gather every-one for a picnic of peace! These tales remind us that caring for na-ture is just as important as caring for each other.

So, when bedtime rolls around and you pull the covers up to your chin, think of the Sikh communi-ty—like a quilt full of colors, sto-ries, and kindness. Whether it's a mouse sharing a crumb or a giant elephant lending a helping trunk, these tales show us that being part of a community means laughing together, helping each other, and making the world a better place—one furry paw at a time.

The Lesson?
Being part of a community is like being a patch in the coziest quilt—every stitch counts! Sikh teachings remind us that when we share, help, and care (even if it's just a tiny crumb or a silly giggle), we help weave a world full of love and light. So be bold, be kind, and remember—you're one bright patch in one big patchwork of love!

Sikh Heroes
Brave and Kind

Bhagat Singh: The Brave Cub with a Big Heart

In a village full of colorful kites and swirling smells of yummy roti, there lived a clever and kind-hearted boy named Bhagat Singh. But Bhagat wasn't your ordinary kid—oh no! People called him "The Fearless Lion" not because he had a mane (he didn't), but because he had a roaring heart full of courage and a laugh that could chase away any worry.

He wasn't loud or bossy. He didn't need a crown or a superhero cape. Bhagat was a hero because he stood up for others, helped when things got tricky, and could turn even the grumpiest donkey into a friend!

One bright afternoon, Bhagat saw an old farmer struggling with a very stubborn donkey named Dholu. Dholu didn't want to work. Nope! He just stood there, munching grass and ignoring everyone. The farmer sighed.

The birds sighed. Even the clouds looked like they were sighing!

But Bhagat grinned and had an idea. "Dholu!" he called out, "Bet you can't beat me in a race!"

Dholu perked up—no one had challenged him before! Off they went, galloping and giggling through the fields. The farmer's plowing got done, Dholu had fun, and Bhagat gave him a big juicy carrot as a thank-you prize. Sometimes, all it takes is a little play to turn a problem into a party!

Soon, Bhagat's adventures were the talk of the village. He became the go-to helper when things went bananas... literally!

One day, a gang of cheeky monkeys stole the villagers' bananas. Panic! Mayhem! Banana-less breakfasts! But Bhagat just chuckled and disappeared into his house.

Moments later... he returned dressed like a GIANT BANANA!

The monkeys stared. Then they shrieked with joy and chased Banana-Bhagat around the mango trees! Everyone laughed until their tummies hurt. The monkeys dropped the stolen fruit, and Bhagat slipped into a pile of peels, giggling. His silly plan saved the day—and taught everyone that laughter is a mighty tool too.

But Bhagat's biggest strength? Kindness.

He loved bringing kids together to play, help others, and dream up big ideas. One day, he gathered his friends and said, "Let's plant a garden that makes everyone smile!"

They got to work—digging, planting, and giggling the whole way. Tomatoes the size of soccer balls! Carrots that looked like curly mustaches! When harvest time came, they didn't keep it to themselves. They shared the veggies with their neighbors, the temple, and even the birds (who stole a few anyway).

The Lesson?

Bhagat Singh showed that being brave doesn't always mean being the strongest. It can mean being the silliest in a banana suit, the kindest with a shovel, or the smartest with a donkey!

With his courage, laughter, and big heart, Bhagat proved that true heroes don't just roar—they also care, share, and play fair.

So, next time you're feeling unsure or need a boost of bravery, just remember Bhagat Singh, the boy who turned kindness into his superpower—and wore a banana suit like a legend.

Mai Bhago

The Warrior Woman

The Warrior with a Giggle and a Goal

A long time ago, in a village full of spinning charkhas and the smell of spicy sabzi, lived a brave Sikh woman named Mai Bhago. But she wasn't your ordinary warrior. No way! Mai Bhago had a sparkle in her eyes, a mighty horse named Mighty Mane, and a heart so big it could wrap around the whole village twice!

She wore armor that shined like the morning sun and tied her turban with pride. But what made her really special? She believed that being brave wasn't just about swords—it was about standing up for what's right, even when your knees feel a little wobbly.

One sunny day, as butterflies fluttered and mangoes ripened in the trees, Mai Bhago heard something troubling. Some of her fellow Sikh soldiers were feeling scared. "We're not sure we can keep fighting," they whispered. "What if we're not strong enough?"

Mai Bhago crossed her arms, raised one eyebrow, and said with a grin, "Not on my watch!"

She climbed up on Mighty Mane and galloped through the village until all her friends had gathered. "Let me tell you something," she said, her voice as steady as a drumbeat. "Courage doesn't come from armor—it comes from your heart. Even a squirrel can be brave when it protects its acorns!"

The soldiers looked at each other ... and slowly, their frowns turned into fierce grins. They stood tall, ready to march forward—not just with weapons, but with wisdom, teamwork, and a few good jokes up their sleeves.

As they prepared for battle, Mai Bhago shouted, "Remember, if you trip, blame it on the grass trying to hug you!" Everyone laughed, even the goats in the field. With each step, the soldiers grew stronger. They weren't afraid anymore—not with Mai Bhago leading the way, her horse trotting proudly, and her heart leading the charge.

The battle came, and oh, it was wild! But between every shout and every charge, there was laughter and encouragement. "You're doing great!" Mai Bhago called. "Also... did anyone else hear that tree squeak, or was it just me?" The soldiers fought bravely, lifted by her energy and silly one-liners.

And guess what? They won!

When the dust settled and peace returned, the village erupted into celebration. Drums boomed, sweets were passed around, and someone even brought out a dancing chicken (who may or may not have known it was dancing). Everyone cheered for Mai Bhago, the warrior who fought with both strength and silliness.

The Lesson?

Mai Bhago taught us that real warriors don't just swing swords—they lift others with kindness, stand up for what's right, and use laughter as their secret superpower. Whether you're riding a horse, carrying a spoon, or telling jokes to your friends, you can be brave too—especially when your heart leads the way.

Guru Gobind Singh

The Hero with a Twist

The Hero with a Smile

A long time ago, in a land of mountains and mango trees, lived a brave and brilliant leader named Guru Gobind Singh. But he wasn't your usual serious hero—oh no! Guru Gobind Singh was a warrior with a twinkle in his eye and a heart full of fun. He believed that learning could come with laughter, and that even the smallest act of kindness could become the greatest adventure.

One rainy day, when the sky was full of grumbles and the ground was too soggy for games, Guru Gobind Singh called all the children together.

"Let's fly kites!" he declared.

"In the rain?" the kids giggled.

"Yes!" he said, holding up twigs and old newspapers. "We'll make our own!"

Soon, the garden was filled with bright, fluttery kites dancing in the stormy wind. "Each kite color means something," he told them. "Blue is for bravery, yellow for joy, green for kindness!" A flock of chirpy birds swooped through the sky, as if they were joining the party. The kites and the birds flew side by side, making the rainy day feel like a flying festival in the clouds.

Another day, while walking through the village, Guru Gobind Singh spotted a scruffy little dog sitting all alone. Its ears drooped and its tummy growled. Instead of walking past, Guru Gobind Singh sat beside the pup and opened his lunchbox. "Everyone deserves a good meal," he said, breaking his bread in two. The dog wagged its tail so fast it looked like a helicopter! From that day on, the dog became his loyal companion, trotting beside him on every adventure—whether it was helping the poor or cheering up someone sad.

But don't think this hero only helped humans! During Vaisakhi, Guru Gobind Singh organized a feast so big, even the forest animals got an invite. There were dancing goats, singing birds, and a cheeky rabbit that did a somersault and landed in a bowl of rice! Everyone clapped and laughed. "Every creature has a gift to share," Guru Gobind Singh said. "That's what makes a community special."

Wherever he went, he shared stories about animals who showed courage, cleverness, and kindness. "The lion is strong," he'd say, "but never forget—the squirrel is quick and the duck is wise! We can all be heroes in our own way."

And oh, how the children loved him! They followed him

through fields and forests, learning through stories, games, and giggles. To them, he was more than a leader—he was a friend who showed that strength and kindness go hand in hand.

The Lesson?

Guru Gobind Singh taught us that being brave doesn't mean being loud, and being kind doesn't mean being quiet. It means sharing your snack with someone who's hungry, helping others smile, and turning even the rainiest day into a rainbow of adventure. Whether you're a kite-flyer, a dancing goat, or just a kid with a big heart—you can be a hero too.

Festivals and Celebrations

Let's Party!

Vaisakhi: A Day of Dancing and Doing Good

In a village full of sunshine and singing birds, a cheerful buzz filled the air. It was Vaisakhi, and everyone was ready to celebrate! Vaisakhi is a joyful harvest festival, a time when farmers smile at their golden fields and say, "Thank you, earth!" It's also a day when Sikh families all over the world remember something extra special—bravery, unity, and the power of sharing.

That morning, little Taran and her cousin Veer raced out of the house in their brightest clothes. Taran wore a sparkly orange salwar kameez, and Veer had a turban that looked like it was made of sunshine.

"Let's go dance!" Veer shouted, spinning in a circle.

Soon, the village square was alive with color. People danced the Bhangra, clapped to dhol drums, and sang with joy. Even the cows in the field looked impressed. One goat tried to join in by hopping side to side—but got so dizzy, it flopped into a haystack! Everyone laughed and clapped. "Now that's a dancing goat!" Taran giggled.

But Vaisakhi isn't only about music and fun—it's a day to remember the creation of the Khalsa, a group of brave Sikhs started by Guru Gobind Singh Ji. He wanted people to stand up for truth, fairness, and kindness. Taran's grandfather sat all the children in a circle under the big mango tree and began one of his famous stories.

"Did I ever tell you about the time a clever monkey helped a Sikh warrior escape from a tricky spot?" he asked, his eyes twinkling.

"Nooo! Tell us!" the kids shouted.

"Well," Grandpa said, "this monkey jumped onto the enemy's head and tossed mangoes everywhere! While the enemies were slipping and sliding, the warrior ran to safety." The kids roared with laughter, imagining the monkey flinging fruit like a superhero.

After the stories, it was time to share food. The Langar tent was filled with families cooking together—stirring pots, flipping rotis, and dishing out sweet kheer. "Pass the rice!" someone called. "More gulab jamun, please!" said another.

Taran helped hand out ladoos to the little ones and offered water to the elders. "Sharing is the best part," she said. "Everyone gets something, and no one is left out."

Even the forest animals joined in the fun. A line of squirrels nibbled on spilled crumbs, and a sneaky puppy was spotted licking a spoon someone dropped. "He's just helping with cleanup!" Veer joked.

As the sun dipped low and painted the sky with pink and gold, families sat together under the stars. They talked about the hard work of the farmers, the courage of the Khalsa, and the joy of coming together.

The Lesson?

Vaisakhi reminds us to celebrate with joy, dance with love, and share with open hearts. Whether you're a dancing goat, a helpful monkey, or a kid with a smile and a spoon, you can make the world brighter—one story, one step, and one sweet treat at a time.

Gurpurab

A Celebration of Light

A Light Full of Love

In a cheerful village filled with singing birds and smiling faces, there came a day when excitement sparkled in the air. It was Gurpurab—the big celebration of Guru Nanak's birthday! But this wasn't any ordinary birthday party. This was the kind where hearts lit up brighter than the lanterns, and everyone—from tiny tots to grandmas with twinkly eyes—joined the fun.

The Gurdwara glowed with glowing lights and colorful flags dancing in the wind. "It looks like the stars came down to visit!" giggled little Meher as she skipped beside her brother Aman. Their whole neighborhood looked like it was having a friendly twinkle-light contest—and no one was losing!

Inside, the sweet sound of singing filled the hall. Everyone clapped along to the hymns, their voices rising like happy birds in the sky.

Even the pigeons outside flapped their wings as if they were singing too!

But Gurpurab wasn't just about music and lights. Oh no—there was food. Lots and lots of it.

The langar kitchen was busy with helpers big and small, all stirring pots and flipping fluffy rotis. There were trays of halwa, bowls of warm kheer, and golden naan stacked so high it almost wobbled like a tower! "This is a feast fit for a lion!" said Uncle Harjit, wiping his hands and laughing.

A clever squirrel peeked in through the window, nose twitching. "I smell ladoos!" he probably thought, sneaking closer to snatch a crumb when no one was looking. But instead of scolding, the children gently offered him a piece. "Even our forest friends should celebrate," said Meher, placing the treat by the door.

After lunch, everyone gathered around to hear stories about Guru Nanak. Grandma Ji told a favorite one about the time Guru Nanak went fishing—but caught a frog instead! "Boing! Boing! Boing!" she said, hopping like the frog and making all the kids laugh until their tummies hurt.

"But what did we learn from it?" she asked, smiling. "That sometimes, unexpected things happen—and we should face them with friendship and a smile."

Later, kids helped decorate the street with paper lanterns and shiny banners. Some hung theirs perfectly... others, well, let's just say the family dog ran off with a streamer and turned it into a tail wiggle parade! "Even silly moments can shine," Aman said, laughing as they chased him down the path.

As the sky turned dark and the stars blinked awake, the village gathered for the Nagar Kirtan, a special walking celebration full of song. People walked side by side, singing with joy, carrying candles and colorful flags. It felt a bit like the forest animals gathering for a nighttime party—everyone together, glowing from the inside out.

The Lesson?

Gurpurab teaches us that true light doesn't come from lamps or lanterns—it comes from love, laughter, and sharing. Just like Guru Nanak did, we can brighten the world with kindness, stories, and silly dances too.

Meher looked up at the stars, holding her brother's hand. "Next Gurpurab," she whispered, "let's invite the whole world."

And with a heart full of joy, the lights of Gurpurab twinkled on—inside and out.

Diwali

The Festival of Lights with a Sikh Twist

Chintu's Diwali Delight

In a forest not too far away, where the fireflies twinkle and the wind hums a happy tune, lived a curious little mouse named Chintu. Chintu had twitchy whiskers, tiny paws, and a big heart that loved any excuse for a celebration. And today? Today was Diwali, the Festival of Lights!

But Chintu's Diwali wasn't about just lighting lamps—it was about something extra special. You see, Sikhs celebrate Diwali in a way that adds a sparkle of bravery and a sprinkle of kindness. Chintu wanted to do it just right.

He scurried through the forest gathering his friends. "Let's light up the night—not just with lamps, but with love!" he squeaked. On his way, he bumped into a wise old owl named Babu, who fluffed his feathers and said, "Real Diwali light comes from helping others, Chintu. That's what Guru Hargobind Ji taught us."

Chintu's ears perked up. "Helping others? I'm in!" he cheered.

And so the animals got to work. The squirrels tied shiny ribbons around tree trunks, the birds hung paper lanterns from branches, and the frogs practiced their best croaks for the evening concert. The whole forest buzzed with excitement—and giggles. Even the grumpy porcupine joined in, carefully stringing up fairy lights (without poking any holes, for once!).

When the sun dipped behind the hills and the stars began to wink, the forest came alive with glowing lights. Everyone gathered under the biggest tree where Babu the owl perched proudly.

"I have a story to share," he hooted. "Long ago, Guru Hargobind Ji bravely stood up for those who were treated unfairly. He didn't just celebrate Diwali with lights—he brought real light into people's lives by freeing the innocent and standing up for what was right."

The animals listened closely, their eyes wide and their hearts full.

Chintu stood up on a toadstool and squeaked, "If Guru Hargobind Ji could do something so brave and kind, then so can we!" Inspired, the animals filled baskets with fruits, nuts, and sweet treats to share with the forest creatures who didn't have much. They tiptoed from burrow to burrow, leaving goodies like secret surprises.

Soon, the raccoons—known for their silly tricks—began breakdancing near the campfire. "Look at them go!" laughed Chintu, wiggling along. "Who knew raccoons could dance like jellybeans on a trampoline?" The whole forest burst into laughter.

As the night slowed down, the animals sat around the crackling fire, munching snacks and swapping stories. Chintu snuggled into a leaf pile, feeling warm and proud.

The Lesson?

Diwali isn't just about lights and sweets—it's about lighting up hearts with kindness, standing tall with bravery, and celebrating together as one big family. That's the Sikh way to shine.

Chintu yawned, his belly full and his heart even fuller. "Next year," he whispered, "we'll invite every-one."

And with that, he drifted off to sleep—dreaming of lanterns, laughter, and the biggest Diwali yet.

The Power of Community

Together We Can!

Langar: The Kitchen of Kindness

In every Gurdwara—the Sikh place of prayer—there's a cozy, wonderful space filled with the smells of warm bread, bubbling curries, and something even sweeter... kindness! This special place is called Langar, the community kitchen, where everyone is welcome to eat, help, and smile together.

In Langar, it doesn't matter if you're big or small, young or old, or even how many samosas you can eat in one sitting—everyone gets a seat at the table. People sit side by side, shoulder to shoulder, just like one big family picnic. And guess what? No one has to pay a penny! It's all made with love and shared with joy.

One busy Sunday, little Harnoor arrived at the Gurdwara with her grandpa. "Are we going to eat today?" she asked excitedly. Grandpa chuckled, "Yes, and we're going to help too!" Harnoor's eyes lit up. She tied on a tiny apron and joined the other helpers in the kitchen. Some were chopping carrots, others were stirring big pots of dal, and Harnoor? She carefully stacked soft, warm rotis into a basket—like golden moons ready to be shared.

Nearby, Uncle Jaspreet was teaching the older kids how to wash dishes without splashing too much (although somehow, someone always ended up with a soggy sleeve). There were giggles, clinks, and the sound of kindness being stirred into every spoonful.

As lunch was served, everyone sat in neat rows on the floor. A shy boy named Aman sat beside a chatty aunty who shared her mango pickle and a funny story about the time her paratha flew off her plate! They laughed and passed bowls down the row, filling each other's plates and hearts.

Even the animals in the courtyard seemed curious. A squirrel peeked through the window, nose twitching. "No acorns?" he seemed to say. But instead, someone gently placed a crumb of roti on the windowsill. The squirrel grabbed it with delight and zipped away—maybe to start his own squirrel-sized Langar!

Langar isn't just about food—it's about seva, or selfless service. It teaches us that helping others is a way to show love, and that sharing a meal means sharing joy. Whether you're sprinkling spices or folding napkins, your hands are helping build something beautiful.

The Lesson?

Langar reminds us that kindness can be cooked, served, and shared. It doesn't matter who you are—when we sit together, eat together, and help together, we become one big family. Sikhism teaches us that when we give with open hands and open hearts, the world becomes a warmer, happier place—one roti at a time.

Kindness in Every Color

In a bright little village where music played and flowers swayed, lived a cheerful girl named Simran. Simran loved two things more than anything—colors and kindness. She had a big basket of crayons and an even bigger heart. Every morning, she would sit outside her house and draw pictures of the people in her village. But Simran didn't just color what she saw—she colored what she felt. If someone was happy, she gave them sunshine yellow. If someone was kind, she drew them in sparkly pink.

One morning, Simran saw her neighbor, Mr. Singh, looking grumpy. His flowers hadn't bloomed, and his teacup was chipped. Simran didn't say a word. Instead, she drew him a beautiful picture of a garden with big blooming marigolds and placed it gently on his doorstep. When Mr. Singh found it, he smiled for the first time all week!

"Well, what a surprise!" he chuckled. "My flowers may be sleeping, but this drawing woke up my heart."

A few days later, Simran saw her friend Harjit looking sad. His kite had gotten stuck in a tree. "Don't worry," Simran said softly, "I'll draw you a new one." She pulled out her crayons and sketched a big red kite with a trail of stars behind it. "You can't fly this one," she said, "but it'll always fly in your imagination!" Harjit beamed. "This is even better!" he shouted. And from that day on, he carried the drawing everywhere, tucked safely in his school bag.

During the festival of Vaisakhi, Simran decided to do something extra special. She set up a little art station outside the Gurdwara, the Sikh place of worship. "Free happy pictures!" her sign read. People lined up—old and young, sleepy and wide awake—and everyone left with a drawing that made them smile. Some pictures had dancing dhol drums, others had golden wheat fields, and one had a giant ladoo with sparkles on top!

The sangat (community) was so impressed that they asked Simran to share why she loved giving so much. Standing on a little stool, she said proudly, "Guru Nanak Ji, the first Sikh Guru, taught us to share, to care, and to see everyone as part of one big family. When we help others—even with something small—it makes their hearts grow and ours too!"

The Lesson?

You don't need money, muscles, or magic to make someone's day better. A kind heart, a bright smile, or even a crayon can be a powerful way to show love. That's what Simran learned—and it's

what Sikhism teaches too: Kindness is a color that never fades.

Helping Hands: Stories of Sikh Service

Helping Hands and Furry Friends

In a bustling village full of chatter and charm, lived a kind-hearted Sikh named Balbir. He had a special gift—he could always find a way to help others, especially animals. Balbir's best friend was a cheeky parrot named Chatterbox, who loved repeating everything he heard.

One bright morning, Balbir spotted a group of naughty monkeys swiping fruits from the neighbor's garden. But instead of getting angry, he came up with a clever plan. He turned to Chatterbox and said, "Why don't you go tell those monkeys that sharing is more fun?" Off flew the parrot, feathers fluttering, squawking loud and clear, "Hey monkeys, let's share the fruits!" The monkeys froze, blinked, and then burst into laughter. After some silly chatter and lots of head-scratching, they agreed to split the fruits with Balbir and Chatterbox—grinning the whole time.

Not far away lived a brave Sikh girl named Amar, who adored animals, especially cows. One day, as she walked through the village with her friends, they spotted a cow stuck knee-deep in a muddy puddle. While her friends posed for selfies, Amar leapt into action. "She needs us! Come on, team!" she shouted. With a few muddy splashes, teamwork, and giggles, they managed to pull the cow out.

She gave a happy "Moo!" and nuzzled Amar in thanks. To celebrate, the kids threw a mini party with crunchy grass and sweet treats. The cow wiggled and twirled with joy—dancing like no one was watching!

In the heart of the village lived Guru Singh, the jolliest storyteller around. His laugh was so loud, it could make birds fly off rooftops! At the Vaisakhi festival, he dressed up as a lion and gathered all the children under the big banyan tree. "Come closer, cubs!" he bellowed in his best lion voice. "A lion protects its family—and we protect our furry friends!" The children squealed with laughter. His stories were full of heroes with tails, hooves, and paws, showing that bravery comes in many shapes—even small, furry ones.

When Gurpurab arrived, the village buzzed with kindness. Families cooked giant pots of food for everyone—including the stray dogs and cats nearby. One mischievous pup, Bholu, had a nose for sweets. One day, he zoomed into the kitchen and ran off with an entire plate of jalebis! The villagers chased him in circles, laughing all the way. When they finally caught him, they couldn't stay mad. "Let's make him his own batch," someone said. And they did—Bholu got his very own treat, proving that kindness often comes wrapped in giggles and wagging tails.

Down by the riverbank lived Tikki, a slow-moving tortoise with a head full of wisdom. Animals often gathered around him, eager for his gentle stories. One peaceful afternoon, Tikki began, "When the river flows, it gives life to everything around it. That's how we should care for each other."

The animals nodded. Inspired, they decided to clean up the river. Squirrels scurried with acorns, ducks waddled with buckets, and frogs sang silly cleanup songs. By sunset, the river sparkled like never before—and so did their hearts.

The Lesson?

Helping hands can lift more than just heavy things—they lift hearts too. Whether you're a lion-hearted storyteller, a brave girl in boots, or even a sweet-toothed dog, your kindness makes the world brighter, cleaner, and a whole lot more fun. T

The Joy of Giving

Sharing is Caring

Momo the Mango Monkey Learns to Share

In a lively little village full of rustling trees and chirping birds, there lived a cheeky monkey named Momo. Now, Momo wasn't just any monkey—he had a special fruit-find-ing nose that could sniff out the juiciest, squishiest, most mango-licious mangoes in the whole jungle! His friends adored him... but Momo had one tiny problem—he didn't like to share.

One bright morning, Momo spotted the biggest mango his eyes had ever seen—round, golden, and glowing like a mini sun! "Mine, mine, all mine!" he squealed, hugging the mango like it was his long-lost twin. He scampered up the tallest tree, ready to munch away in peace.

Down below, Chikki the giggly parrot flapped her wings and called out, "Hey Momo! That mango looks AMAZING! Can we have a bite?"

Beside her, Baba Tortoise the wise old turtle smiled and added, "You know, Momo, sharing that mango might just make it taste even better!"

Momo scrunched up his nose. "No way! I found it, and it's mine. Sharing's for squirrels!"

Baba Turtu chuckled, "Ah, little m onkey... even a squirrel knows the joy of giving."

Momo rolled his eyes, took a big juicy bite—and SQUISH! Mango juice dribbled down his chin, all sticky and sweet. He looked at his enormous mango and suddenly realized... it was way too big for one little monkey tummy.

"Okay, fine! Maybe just one bite each," he huffed. But as soon as Chikki and Baba Turtu took their bites, something magical happened...

The mango party began!
Chikki squawked silly jokes, Baba Turtu shared funny stories from his tortoise-y teenage years, and Momo? He laughed so hard mango came out of his nose (ew, but funny!). They munched and gig-

gled, turning one mango into a memory full of joy.

As the sun dipped low and fireflies twinkled above, Momo looked around at his happy, mango-covered friends and smiled. "This is the BEST mango ever," he said. "Not because it's big—but because I shared it with you!"

From that day on, Momo wasn't just the jungle's best fruit finder—he became known as "Momo the Mango Monkey Who Shares Everything!" Mangoes, bananas, silly jokes, hugs—you name it!

And just like the Sikh teachings remind us, kindness grows when it's shared, and a joyful heart is the tastiest treat of all.

So next time you find something special—like a cookie, a crayon, or a cozy spot on the couch—remember Momo's mango and let the joy of sharing make your day even sweeter!

The Lesson?

Sharing isn't just about giving away your stuff—it's about making memories, spreading joy, and growing your heart a little bigger each time. Whether it's a juicy mango or a silly story, when you share with others, everyone—including you—feels happier inside. Sikh wisdom teaches us that kindness is one of the greatest gifts we can give. And just like Momo learned, a little sharing can turn an ordinary moment into a magical one.

Nature and Sikh Teachings

The Guru's Garden

Nature's Classroom

In a cheerful little village wrapped in blossoms and bird songs, there was a magical garden looked after by a wise and smiley old guru. This wasn't just any garden—it was a wonderland where animals played nicely, flowers swayed to the breeze, and learning felt like an adventure. Every morning, the guru would plop down under a big shady tree (his glasses always sliding down his nose!) and call out, "Welcome to the best classroom in the whole wide world—my garden!"

One sunny morning, the children gathered with curious eyes and twitchy noses, just in time to spot a sneaky little fox poking his head out from a bush. "Ah, that clever fox," the guru chuckled. "He teaches us that being smart and thinking before we act can help solve big problems—just like when you can't reach a cookie on the top shelf and need a clever plan!" The fox gave the children a sly wink, making everyone giggle and whisper, "He really is a smarty-paws!"

Next, the guru waddled over (his robes always tripping on daisies!) to a circle of bouncing rabbits happily munching on crunchy carrots. "Look at these little guys," he grinned. "They remind us how lovely it is to share. Like during Vaisakhi, when we share food, fun, and smiles with everyone around." Just then, one fluffy rabbit pushed his carrot toward another, and the kids clapped. "Aww! Bunny buddies!"

Then came the tallest tree in the garden, where Mr. Owl sat with serious eyes and a very important face. "Meet Mr. Owl," said the guru, lowering his voice to match the owl's wisdom. "He teaches us about looking after others. Just like the Sikh community helps people in need, Mr. Owl keeps watch over all the tiny creatures here to keep them safe." The owl gave a proud hoot, and the children nodded as if they were being let in on a very wise secret.

As the sun began to dip low, painting the garden golden, the guru gathered the children close. "Nature is like a giant storybook," he said gently. "If we listen closely, the animals and plants whisper lessons about kindness, bravery, and caring for one another." The children smiled, some even hugged the trees goodbye (and one tried to hug the fox, but he darted off playfully). They skipped away, their hearts full of garden giggles and new wisdom.

The Lesson?

Even the tiniest creatures in nature can be our teachers. If we watch closely and listen with kind hearts, we'll learn how to be clever like the fox, generous like the rabbits, and caring like Mr. Owl. Just like in the Sikh faith, the world becomes brighter when we share, help, and learn together!

Animals in Sikh Teachings

Friends of the Earth

Animal Buddies & Sikh Wisdom

In a cozy village where the sun smiled and the birds sang sweet songs, there lived the silliest squirrel named Chaitanya. Chaitanya wasn't just any squirrel—he had the speed of a zooming rocket and a giggle that made even the grumpiest goat chuckle. Every morning, he zipped around the gurdwara courtyard, gathering shiny nuts and peeking in on the kids playing tag. One day, Chaitanya couldn't resist and joined the game! He dashed through the giggling group, tail swishing, while the children tried to catch him. Spoiler alert: they never did! Chaitanya's cheeky chase reminded everyone that animals love to play and be part of our fun too.

Nearby, perched in a big old tree, lived Babu the owl—wise, wrinkly, and always wearing his imaginary glasses. Babu loved sunset storytime. When the sky turned orange and sleepy, he gathered his friends—Chaitanya the zooming squirrel, Rani the bouncy rabbit, and Moti the floppy-eared dog. With a gentle hoot, he shared tales of kindness and teamwork. "Whether you fly, hop, bark, or talk," Babu would say, "helping others makes the world sparkle a little brighter!" The animals all nodded with their paws, wings, and tails. They knew Babu's words were the real deal.

Now, let's talk about the trickster of the garden—Miku the monkey! Miku had a nose for mischief and a serious sweet tooth. During the big Vaisakhi celebration, he tiptoed (well, tip-jumped) into the gurdwara kitchen and spotted a giant plate of ladoos. "Ooooh, treasure!" he squeaked. But instead of gobbling them all up, he shared them with Chaitanya, Babu, Rani, and Moti. Soon, the furry friends were having a side-splitting sweet party under the mango tree. They danced, laughed, and learned that sharing sweets makes them even sweeter—just like in Sikh traditions, where sharing brings everyone closer.

Little Raju, the curious puppy, wasn't far behind. He loved sniffing around the flower garden, chasing butterflies (but never catching them), and digging tiny holes. One day, he spotted a sparkly blue butterfly. Instead of jumping after it, Raju sat still and watched it dance through the air. "Wow," he whispered, "even tiny wings can make big beauty." From that day on, Raju made sure not to squish the ants, scare the bees, or tug on flower petals. He became the garden's gentle guardian, learning that respecting nature is a way to show love to the whole world—just like Sikh teachings say!

Together, this furry gang taught big lessons through small paws. They giggled, played, helped each other, and showed that animals can be some of the wisest friends we'll ever have. Whether you're swinging like Miku or snoozing like Babu, there's always a little Sikh wisdom hidden in every animal tale.

The Lesson?

Animals may not speak like us, but their actions are filled

with kindness, fun, and wisdom. In Sikh teachings, every creature matters—whether you chirp, bark, or giggle. By watching our furry friends, we learn to play fair, share joy, care for the Earth, and spread love wherever we go!

Protecting Our Planet

Sikh Values and Nature

Furry Friends Save the Day!

In a sunny park filled with wiggly worms and whispering leaves, there lived a cheeky little squirrel named Chintu. Chintu had a big fluffy tail and an even bigger heart. He spent his days zooming between trees, collecting shiny acorns—not just for himself, but for all his squirrel buddies too! "One for me, one for you, and one for the chipmunk down the hill!" he'd squeak. Chintu believed in sharing, just like the Sikh Gurus taught. "Sharing is caring," he chirped, "and also way more fun!" Because let's face it—snacks are better when you don't eat them alone.

Now, flying high above the trees was Pappi the parrot, the noisiest bird in the whole village. Pappi wasn't just loud—he was also super passionate about trees!

"Squawk! Don't cut down our leafy pals!" he'd shout from the top of the gurdwara. He'd flap in circles anytime someone got too close to a tree with clippers. "Trees give shade, homes, and air for your nose!" he'd holler. Pappi may have been a bit dramatic (and a little bossy), but he taught everyone that trees aren't just decorations—they're part of our big green family!

On festival days like Vaisakhi, the whole animal crew got into the party spirit! Imagine fluffy rabbits wearing flower necklaces, hopping in line with brooms in their paws. "Let's clean up and cele-brate!" they cheered. With music playing and carrots as snacks, the rabbits danced their way around the park, picking up litter and making the place sparkle. "Keeping things clean is part of the party," said one bunny with a glittery bowtie. And just like that, cleaning up became a hop-hop-hooray kind of fun!

Now picture this—every animal in the forest holding a wild jungle meeting! Mr. Elephant, the bossy-but-wise speaker, stood tall while cheeky monkeys threw peanuts in the air. "We must protect our jungle home!" he trumpeted. The monkeys, ants, birds, and even the sleepy sloth clapped their paws and claws. "Every little creature counts!" shouted a mouse from under a leaf. They all agreed: teamwork makes the trees grow tall and the rivers run clear. And the meeting ended in a giant group hug (well, except for the porcupine—he got a high-five instead).

Whether it's Chintu the generous squirrel, Pappi the parrot with a loud mouth and a green mission, or a forest full of silly critters working together, one thing is clear—Sikh values help us take care of our world with love, laughter, and leafy green hearts.

The Lesson?

Nature needs us, and we need nature! Sikh teachings remind us to share, protect, and care—not just for people, but for every furry, feathery, and fluttery friend too. So next time you see a squirrel, a tree, or even a tiny ant, remember—you're part of their team, and together, you can make the world a cleaner, greener, happier place!

Animal Tales

Fables with a Lesson

Miko the Monkey and the Fruit Salad Fiasco

In a cheerful little village full of giggles, goats, and gossiping parrots, there lived a mischievous monkey named Miko. Miko was famous for two things: his banana-juggling skills and his hilarious pranks. He could swing through trees with his eyes closed (although he didn't recommend it), and he once made a whole group of chickens dance by flapping banana peels like tambourines. But Miko had one dream—he wanted to impress the wise old Guru who told the best stories under the big banyan tree.

One sunny afternoon, Miko heard the Guru talking to a bunch of kids about bravery, kindness, and helping others. "Pfft," Miko whispered to himself, "I can be brave, kind, and hilarious!" So he decided it was time for a show-stopping entrance.

He gathered bananas, apples, grapes, even some slightly squishy strawberries, and made a huge fruit mountain. Then—**SPLAT!**—he leaped from a tree and landed right in the middle of it. Fruit flew everywhere. "Ta-da! I'm a fruit salad!" Miko yelled, striking a dramatic pose with a pineapple hat on his head.

The children burst into giggles. The Guru smiled too, but not because of the fruit hat. "Well, well, Miko," he said, adjusting his turban. "A very colorful... performance. But tell me, what's the most important fruit in your sal-ad?"

Miko blinked. "Uh... bananas? Def-initely bananas. They're funny, they're bendy, and they go squish when you sit on them!" he replied proudly. The Guru chuckled and said, "Yes, bananas are funny. But every fruit in that salad adds something special. Life's like that too—everyone brings their own flavor."

Miko scratched his fuzzy head. "So... you're saying even a grape matters?"

"Exactly!" the Guru said. "Big or

small, squishy or round, everyone has something valuable to share."

Miko jumped up, tossing an orange to a laughing kid. "Then I want to be the best team-fruit ever!" he shouted. From that day on, Miko became the village's giggle-giver and helper-extraordinaire. He still played pranks (very harmless and very silly), but he also helped carry baskets, find lost sandals, and even taught a duck how to juggle peas.

The Guru often smiled and said, "Miko's not just clever—he's clever with kindness," and told his tale whenever kids needed a little nudge to play nice and stick together.

The Lesson?

Being funny is great, and being clever is cool—but the real magic happens when you use your silliness, smarts, and heart to help others. Just like a fruit salad, life is better when everyone brings their best and shares it with joy!

The Brave Elephant and the Kind-hearted Sikh

B haloo the Brave and the Cart in the Ditch

In a bright, bustling village where mangoes dropped with a plop!

and butterflies danced like confetti, lived a big, gentle elephant named Bhaloo. Now, Bhaloo wasn't just any elephant—oh no! He had the floppiest ears, the fluffiest tail, and the kindest heart in the whole jungle side of Punjab. His bird and monkey friends loved to giggle, "Bhaloo, with those big ears, you might just fly away one day!" But Bhaloo only chuckled. He didn't mind the teasing—he knew kindness made you strong on the inside.

One sunny afternoon, while chomping on juicy mangoes under his favorite tree, Bhaloo heard a ker-thump! and lots of shouting. "Trouble!" he trumpeted, and off he trotted to find out what was going on.

At the edge of the village, he saw a big mess! A wooden cart had tumbled into a muddy ditch, and no matter how hard the villagers tried, it just wouldn't budge. Standing nearby was a cheerful Sikh named Amar, puffing and huffing, trying his best to lift one wheel.

Bhaloo's ears perked up, and his tail gave a determined wiggle. "Step aside, everyone! Elephant muscles reporting for duty!" he called. With a big oomph! and a little wiggle-wiggle, Bhaloo wrapped his strong trunk around the cart and—whoosh!—up it came!

"Hooray!" the villagers cheered. Amar clapped his hands and laughed, "Bhaloo, you're the hero of the day!" Bhaloo bashfully shuffled his feet (which was hard for such a big fellow) and said, "Helping friends is what I do best!"

But wait! Just when everyone was about to celebrate, a tiny meow! came from above. Up in a tree, a kitten clung to a skinny branch, looking as wobbly as jelly on a spoon.

"Oh no!" gasped Amar. "We need a plan!"

Quick as a blink, Bhaloo knelt down and lifted Amar onto his back. Up, up, up they went—closer to the mewing fluffball. Amar reached out gently, and with a careful nudge from Bhaloo's trunk, the kitten was safe and sound in Amar's arms. The villagers clapped again, even louder than before!

That evening, the whole village had a big picnic. There were laddoos, rotis, giggles, and hugs. Amar and Bhaloo sat under the stars, sharing their favorite mangoes and stories of their silly, brave day.

The Lesson?

Helping others—big or small—is always the right thing to do. Just like in Sikh teachings, kindness, teamwork, and standing up to help with courage turn ordinary days into extraordinary adventures. Whether you're a fluffy-tailed elephant or a smiley-hearted human, being brave and kind makes the world a better place!

The Loyal Dog

A Tale of Friendship

Arjun and Poochie's Festival Feast

In a cozy little village nestled among golden fields, lived a cheerful boy named Arjun and his bouncy best friend—a scruffy little dog named Poochie. Poochie's tail wagged so fast, it looked like a helicopter ready for takeoff!

Every morning, as Arjun packed his schoolbag, Poochie bounced in circles, barking, "Let's go, let's go—adventure awaits!"

These two were the ultimate dream team. They shared snacks (even the crunchy ones), told secrets under the mango tree, and had their own special hand-shake—which mostly involved a lot of giggles and tail-wagging.

One sunny afternoon, Arjun and Poochie stumbled upon a group of kids decorating for the up-coming Vaisakhi festival. Color-ful kites danced in the wind, and everyone was buzzing with excitement. Poochie wasted no time—he leaped into the fun, chasing ribbons, rolling in the grass, and even untangling a string (well, kind of). "You're the best festival helper ever!" Arjun laughed. "You deserve a gold medal made of roti!"

The kids roared with laughter, and Poochie gave a proud bark, striking a superhero pose.

But the villagers had a little problem—there weren't enough veggies for the big community feast! "We need more food if everyone's going to eat," someone sighed. Arjun's eyes lit up. "Poochie, it's veg-gie-mission time!"

Off they went! Poochie sniffed out the crunchiest cucumbers and roundest tomatoes, while Arjun carried a basket, cheering him on. They came back covered in dirt, giggling and proud. "Veggie he-roes reporting for duty!" Arjun de-clared, holding up a carrot like a sword.

Festival day arrived with music, dancing, and mountains of yum-my food. Poochie, tail wagging like a drumbeat, watched the plates being passed around. Ar-jun whispered, "Sharing is a big part of being Sikh, buddy. Even you can do it!" Just then, a kind aunty tossed Poochie a warm piece of roti. He caught it mid-air, wagged his tail, and shared a lick with the smallest puppy in town.

The villagers clapped and cheered. "Hooray for Arjun and Poochie!" someone shouted. Their loyalty, teamwork, and giggles had brought everyone together.

As the sun dipped below the fields and the kites floated like dreams in the sky, Arjun snuggled beside his fluffy best friend. "Poochie," he whispered, "you're not just my dog. You're my most loyal pal." Poochie barked once, softly, as if to say, "And you're my forever human."

The Lesson?

True friendship means showing up for each other, helping where we can, and always sharing what we have—even if it's just a tail wag or a roti crumb. Just like in Sikhism, being loyal and generous makes every day feel like a festival of love.

Imaginative Sikh Tales

The Magical Turban

Miko's Turban Time-Trip

In a sunny little village tucked between bouncy green hills, lived a cheeky monkey named Miko. Now, Miko wasn't just any monkey—oh no! He had a bright red turban that sparkled like fireflies at midnight. Some said it was magical. Others said it was just very glittery. But Miko? He believed it could take him on the coolest adventure ever!

One afternoon, while munching a banana (as all great monkey stories begin), Miko gave his turban a wiggle, a twist, and a giggle, and wished aloud, "I wanna meet a Sikh hero!" And poof! faster than you can say "jalebi jumble," Miko zipped through time and landed right in the middle of Amritsar—busy, buzzing, and glowing with the shimmer of the Golden Temple!

There, Miko spotted a kind man with a giant water jug: Bhai Kanhaiya! He was giving water to everyone—even the people on the other team during a big battle. Miko's eyes widened like saucers. "He's helping everybody?" Just then, a curious parrot flew by and pecked at Bhai Kanhaiya's jug, thinking it was a juicy coconut! SPLASH! Water everywhere! Miko laughed so hard he rolled over. But his monkey heart felt warm too. "Whoa," he whispered, "that's what real kindness looks like."

Twist! Wiggle! Giggle! Off Miko flew again—this time straight into

the middle of a Vaisakhi celebration! Music thumped, colors swirled, and ohhh the food!
Miko, always ready for a good
time, tried the bhangra dance...
but tripped over his own tail and
splat! landed right into a plate
of syrupy jalebis. Covered in sug-
ar and giggling, he licked his fingers and thought, "Festivals are
the best when you share joy—and
snacks!"

Next stop? A big day of
sewa—helping the community!
People were cooking food, sharing clothes, and planting trees.
Miko wanted to help too, so

he grabbed a bunch of bananas to plant...except instead of digging holes, he flung them like boomerangs. BONK! The village cows caught every banana like pros and mooed in approval. "Okay," Miko shrugged, "maybe I'm better at feeding cows than planting trees."

And just when Miko thought he'd seen it all, the turban gave one final twist!—and whoosh! he was in a peaceful forest full of talking animals! A wise old tortoise was telling stories about Guru Nanak and how he taught love for every living being. The owl hooted she was the wisest because she could see at night. The rabbit thumped his foot—"I'm fastest!" But Miko, tail twitching, stood up and said, "The wisest ones are kindest to everyone, no matter how big or small."

The animals all went quiet. Then they nodded. Then they clapped. (Well, as best as animals can.)

Miko returned home with sticky fur, sparkly eyes, and a heart full of love. His magical turban had taken him on the journey of a lifetime—not just through time, but through the best parts of Sikhism:

kindness, courage, fun, and helping one another.

The Lesson?

Kindness, courage, and community never go out of style—whether
you're dancing in jalebi syrup,
handing out water, or accidental-
ly feeding cows bananas! Just like
Miko learned, Sikh teachings remind us that every act of goodness—big or small—is part of the
greatest adventure of all.

The Flying Khanda

Adventures in the Sky

Kiki the Flying Khanda

Way up in the twinkly skies of Amritsar, there zipped a tee-ny-tiny bird with a BIG sparkle and an even BIGGER mission. Her name? Kiki. But she wasn't just any bird—nope! Kiki looked just like a Khanda, the shining Sikh symbol of strength and unity. With golden feathers that shimmered like sunshine and a silver tail shaped like a little sword, Kiki flapped through the clouds leaving a trail of sparkly stardust wherever she flew.

But Kiki wasn't flying around just for fun—oh no. She had a secret plan. She wanted to teach everyone the coolest thing ever: **Sikh values!**

One bright morning, while doing somersaults over the Golden Temple, Kiki spotted some kids fussing under a big tree. "I'm the best climber!" one shouted. "No way, I am!" said another.

Swoosh! In zipped Kiki, landing with a sparkle and a squawk. "Why argue, when you can team-work?" she chirped. "Climbing is great, but sharing the view from the top? Even better!"

The kids blinked. "How do we do that?"

Kiki flapped her wings and giggled, "One climbs, the others cheer, then switcheroo!" Soon, laughter echoed through the streets as the kids took turns, cheering louder with every climb.

Kiki beamed. "Another friendship mission—complete!"

Later that afternoon, while soaring over golden wheat fields, Kiki spotted a grumbly farmer huffing and puffing as he dragged a big bundle of hay.

"Phew!" he groaned. "This is heavy!"

Zoom! Kiki zipped down. "Mr. Farmer! Why carry that all alone when your neighbors are just a shout away?"

The farmer chuckled. "Good point, little sparkle-feathers!" So he hollered for help—and like magic, folks came running. They sang, they laughed, they hauled hay together like one big happy team.

Kiki did a little loop-de-loop in the air. "That's what I call sewa—community spirit!"

As evening tiptoed in, Kiki heard giggles and chatter from the village square. Kids were getting ready for Vaisakhi, but their float decorations were looking a little… wonky.

"Need some pizzazz?" Kiki asked, landing with flair. "Why not build a float shaped like… ME!"

The kids gasped, then grinned. Flowers, fairy lights, shiny paper—they turned a plain old cart into a flying-Khanda float full of joy and sparkle. When the parade started, Kiki flew above them, glowing like a star, while the whole village clapped and danced below.

That night, Kiki snuggled into her favorite tree branch, her wings tired but her heart full.

"I helped friends work together, share, celebrate, and smile. Not bad for one sparkly bird," she whispered, twirling one last loop before bedtime.

The Lesson?

Kiki taught us that even the smallest feathered friend can spread the biggest love. Sikh values—like teamwork, helping others, and celebrating together—make every day feel like a parade. So be brave, be kind, and remember: you don't need wings to lift others up!

The Singing Sikh

A Voice Like No Other

G urmukh's Great Animal Sing-Along

In a cheerful little village tucked between giggly hills and swishy trees, lived a jolly Sikh named Bhai Gurmukh. But Gurmukh wasn't just known for his shiny turban and kind smile—nope! He had a voice so magical that even animals couldn't resist joining in. Mooing cows, bleating goats, barking dogs—even the grumpy cat from the gurdwara kitchen—sang along whenever Gurmukh opened his mouth!

Every morning, Gurmukh would clear his throat, stretch his arms, and sing out a "Waheguruuuuu!" so tuneful it made the birds tap dance on the rooftops.

One sunny morning, as Gurmukh hummed a silly banana tune, he spotted a grouchy monkey frowning from the tallest tree. "Ahem,"

Gurmukh grinned, "let's turn that frown upside down!" With a wink, he burst into a goofy monkey-jungle melody.

The monkey blinked. Then blinked again. Then—SWING!—he zipped down, made the silliest face ever, and added a series of squeaky "ooh-ooh-ahh-ahhs" that had the whole village in stitches! Even the serious school principal laughed so hard his pagri nearly popped off.

From that moment, Monkey became Gurmukh's number one backup dancer.

News of the singing Sikh and his animal band spread far and wide, and Gurmukh had an idea. "Let's have a show! A HUGE one! With snacks and songs and tail-wagging talent!"

So, he announced: **"The Great Singing Festival of Animals!"**
The village went bananas. Literally. (Monkey may have gone overboard.)

Everyone pitched in—stringing flowers, setting up stages, and teaching parrots how to sing backup. Even the local goats practiced their harmonies!

When the big day came, the village square sparkled with bright colors and the smell of warm samosas. Gurmukh stood proudly at the center, took a deep breath, and sang the first note.

Moo! Woof! Meow! Baaa! From every corner, animals joined in. A sheep even hit a high note so perfectly it made the pots rattle. But the grand finale? That was Monkey—he flipped, he danced, he slid across the stage like a furry superstar!

The crowd clapped and laughed and sang along. Everyone—big,

small, furry, or feathered—was part of one happy, musical family.

As the sun dipped behind the hills, Gurmukh looked at the smiling faces around him. His heart felt so warm it could've melted a ladoo.

The Lesson?

Gurmukh reminded everyone that the best songs are the ones we sing together. Sikh teachings tell us that joy, kindness, and community make life shine. Whether you sing like a nightingale or squeak like a squirrel, your voice matters—and when we lift each other up, the whole world sings in harmony.

Waheguru ji ka Khalsa, Waheguru ji ki Fateh!

The Final Tale: Your Turn, Little Lionheart!

Well well well... look who's still here! You did it, superstar! You've read your way through tales of singing goats, heroic elephants, dancing monkeys, and one seriously fabulous flying Khanda. If your fingers aren't tired from turning pages, your cheeks are probably sore from smiling. So go on—give yourself a giant high-five, or better yet, do the victory chicken dance. (No, seriously. We'll wait.)

Okay! Now let's take a big breath and think back on all the magic you discovered.

You've journeyed through colorful festivals, helped hungry villagers, rescued kittens from trees, and even planted bananas in the name of seva (service)!

And through it all, you've learned that Sikhism isn't just about golden temples or yummy langar meals (although, let's admit it—the roti was chef's kiss). It's about kindness, courage, equality, and showing up for each other—whether you're a monkey with a mischievous streak or a squirrel with snack-stealing skills.

Remember Guru Nanak Dev Ji? The explorer with the big heart and even bigger questions? He taught us that everyone matters. And those amazing Sikh heroes—like the fearless Mai Bhago or Guru Gobind Singh Ji with his lion's heart—showed us that standing up for others is what real bravery looks like. Even if your legs go wobbly or your turban's a bit crooked, you still do the right thing.

Let's not forget the animals! From wise owls who see everything (even when you sneak that cookie), to helpful dogs and dancing parrots—they reminded us that every creature is part of the story, and everyone has something to teach.

But wait! This isn't goodbye. Nope, not even close.

Here's your next big mission, little legend: Be the hero of your own story.

Help a friend. Share your snacks. Make someone laugh with your best goat impression. Stand up for someone who feels small. Hug your nana. Water a tree. Sing loudly—even if you only know half the words.

These small things? They're the biggest things of all.

And if you ever find yourself at a Sikh celebration—like Vaisakhi or Gurpurab—don't hold back! Dance like your feet have fireworks. Eat like your tummy has a second floor. And laugh like the whole animal kingdom is watching (because honestly, they probably are).

So here we are, at the last page... but only of this book.
Because Sikhism? It's not just something you read about.
It's something you live.

The Lesson?
You don't need a magical turban, a talking animal, or a tree that sings to be a hero. You already have everything you need—your heart, your courage, and your

big, beautiful spirit. Sikh teachings show us that the world becomes brighter every time you choose kindness, stand up for others, and treat every creature like family. So go out there and sparkle, superstar.

Waheguru Ji Ka Khalsa, Waheguru Ji Ki Fateh!
(That's our way of saying: "Go change the world, brave one!")

Let's Meet
Psalm

Psalm Carnoustie is a passionate children's author dedicated to introducing young readers to the vibrant world of cultures, religions, and timeless wisdom from around the globe. With a warm and engaging storytelling style, Psalm crafts tales that spark curiosity, foster understanding, and celebrate diversity.

Believing that children are the seeds of a more compassionate future, Psalm is driven by the philosophy that early exposure to different beliefs and traditions nurtures empathy, kindness, and open-mindedness. Her books serve as gentle guides, helping children see the beauty in differences while embracing the common threads that unite us all.

When she's not weaving enchanting stories, Psalm enjoys exploring cultural festivals, collecting folklore from faraway lands, and sharing moments of quiet reflection in nature. Her stories are not just books—they are bridges, connecting little hearts to a world of understanding and acceptance.

www.ingramcontent.com/pod-product-compliance
Lightning Source LLC
LaVergne TN
LVHW051058080426
835508LV00019B/1954